Name of Look _____

Evening ○
Daytime ○

Face
Moisturizer

_____

Concealer

_____

Foundation

_____

Highlight/Blush

_____

Eyes

Brows

_____

Eyelid

_____

Liner

_____

Crease

_____

Mascara

_____

Lips

Liner

_____

Lip Color

_____

Gloss

_____

Notes

I0503636

Name of Look _____

Evening ◯
Daytime ◯

Face
Moisturizer

Concealer

Foundation

Highlight/Blush

Eyes
Brows

Eyelid

Liner

Crease

Mascara

Lips
Liner

Lip Color

Gloss

Notes

Name of Look _____

Evening ○
Daytime ○

Face

Moisturizer

_____

Concealer

_____

Foundation

_____

Highlight/Blush

_____

Eyes

Brows

_____

Eyelid

_____

Liner

_____

Crease

_____

Mascara

_____

Lips

Liner

_____

Lip Color

_____

Gloss

_____

Notes

Name of Look _____

Evening ○
Daytime ○

Face

Moisturizer

_____

Concealer

_____

Foundation

_____

Highlight/Blush

_____

Eyes

Brows

_____

Eyelid

_____

Liner

_____

Crease

_____

Mascara

_____

Lips

Liner

_____

Lip Color

_____

Gloss

_____

Notes

Name of Look _____

Evening ○
Daytime ○

Face

Moisturizer

_____

Concealer

_____

Foundation

_____

Highlight/Blush

_____

Eyes

Brows

_____

Eyelid

_____

Liner

_____

Crease

_____

Mascara

_____

Lips

Liner

_____

Lip Color

_____

Gloss

_____

Notes

Name of Look _____

Evening ◯
Daytime ◯

Face
Moisturizer

_____

Concealer

_____

Foundation

_____

Highlight/Blush

_____

Eyes
Brows

_____

Eyelid

_____

Liner

_____

Crease

_____

Mascara

_____

Lips
Liner

_____

Lip Color

_____

Gloss

_____

Notes

Name of Look _____

Evening ○
Daytime ○

Face

Moisturizer

Concealer

Foundation

Highlight/Blush

Eyes

Brows

Eyelid

Liner

Crease

Mascara

Lips

Liner

Lip Color

Gloss

Notes

Name of Look _____

Evening ○
Daytime ○

Face

Moisturizer
_____

Concealer
_____

Foundation
_____

Highlight/Blush
_____

Eyes

Brows
_____

Eyelid
_____

Liner
_____

Crease
_____

Mascara
_____

Lips

Liner
_____

Lip Color
_____

Gloss
_____

Notes

Name of Look _____

Evening ⚪
Daytime ⚪

Face

Moisturizer

_____

Concealer

_____

Foundation

_____

Highlight/Blush

_____

Eyes

Brows

_____

Eyelid

_____

Liner

_____

Crease

_____

Mascara

_____

Lips

Liner

_____

Lip Color

_____

Gloss

_____

Notes

Name of Look _____

Evening ○
Daytime ○

Face

Moisturizer

_____

Concealer

_____

Foundation

_____

Highlight/Blush

_____

Eyes

Brows

_____

Eyelid

_____

Liner

_____

Crease

_____

Mascara

_____

Lips

Liner

_____

Lip Color

_____

Gloss

_____

Notes

Name of Look _____

Evening ○
Daytime ○

Face

Moisturizer

_____

Concealer

_____

Foundation

_____

Highlight/Blush

_____

Eyes

Brows

_____

Eyelid

_____

Liner

_____

Crease

_____

Mascara

_____

Lips

Liner

_____

Lip Color

_____

Gloss

_____

Notes

Name of Look _____

Evening ○
Daytime ○

Face
Moisturizer

_____

Concealer

_____

Foundation

_____

Highlight/Blush

_____

Eyes
Brows

_____

Eyelid

_____

Liner

_____

Crease

_____

Mascara

_____

Lips
Liner

_____

Lip Color

_____

Gloss

_____

Notes

Name of Look _____

Evening ○
Daytime ○

Face
Moisturizer

Concealer

Foundation

Highlight/Blush

Eyes   **Lips**
Brows   Liner

Eyelid   Lip Color

Liner   Gloss

Crease

Mascara

Notes

Name of Look _____

Evening ○
Daytime ○

Face
Moisturizer

_____

Concealer

_____

Foundation

_____

Highlight/Blush

_____

Eyes
Brows

_____

Eyelid

_____

Liner

_____

Crease

_____

Mascara

_____

Lips
Liner

_____

Lip Color

_____

Gloss

_____

Notes

Name of Look _____

Evening ○
Daytime ○

Face
Moisturizer

_____

Concealer

_____

Foundation

_____

Highlight/Blush

_____

Eyes   **Lips**
Brows   Liner

_____   _____

Eyelid   Lip Color

_____   _____

Liner   Gloss

_____   _____

Crease

_____

Mascara

_____

Notes

Name of Look _____

Evening ◯
Daytime ◯

Face
Moisturizer

_____

Concealer

_____

Foundation

_____

Highlight/Blush

_____

Eyes   **Lips**
Brows   Liner

_____   _____

Eyelid   Lip Color

_____   _____

Liner   Gloss

_____   _____

Crease

_____

Mascara

_____

Notes

Name of Look _____

Evening ◯
Daytime ◯

Face

Moisturizer

_____

Concealer

_____

Foundation

_____

Highlight/Blush

_____

Eyes

Brows

_____

Eyelid

_____

Liner

_____

Crease

_____

Mascara

_____

Lips

Liner

_____

Lip Color

_____

Gloss

_____

Notes

Name of Look _____

Evening ○
Daytime ○

Face
Moisturizer

_____

Concealer

_____

Foundation

_____

Highlight/Blush

_____

Eyes
Brows

_____

Eyelid

_____

Liner

_____

Crease

_____

Mascara

_____

Lips
Liner

_____

Lip Color

_____

Gloss

_____

Notes

Name of Look _____

Evening ○
Daytime ○

Face
Moisturizer

_____

Concealer

_____

Foundation

_____

Highlight/Blush

_____

Eyes
Brows

_____

Eyelid

_____

Liner

_____

Crease

_____

Mascara

_____

Lips
Liner

_____

Lip Color

_____

Gloss

_____

Notes

Name of Look _____

Evening ○
Daytime ○

Face
Moisturizer
_____

Concealer
_____

Foundation
_____

Highlight/Blush
_____

Eyes
Brows
_____

Eyelid
_____

Liner
_____

Crease
_____

Mascara
_____

Lips
Liner
_____

Lip Color
_____

Gloss
_____

Notes

Name of Look _____

Evening ○
Daytime ○

Face

Moisturizer

_____

Concealer

_____

Foundation

_____

Highlight/Blush

_____

Eyes

Brows

_____

Eyelid

_____

Liner

_____

Crease

_____

Mascara

_____

Lips

Liner

_____

Lip Color

_____

Gloss

_____

Notes

Name of Look _____

Evening ◯
Daytime ◯

Face

Moisturizer

_____

Concealer

_____

Foundation

_____

Highlight/Blush

_____

Eyes

Brows

_____

Eyelid

_____

Liner

_____

Crease

_____

Mascara

_____

Lips

Liner

_____

Lip Color

_____

Gloss

_____

Notes

Name of Look _____

Evening ◯
Daytime ◯

Face

Moisturizer

_____

Concealer

_____

Foundation

_____

Highlight/Blush

_____

Eyes

Brows

_____

Eyelid

_____

Liner

_____

Crease

_____

Mascara

_____

Lips

Liner

_____

Lip Color

_____

Gloss

_____

Notes

Name of Look _____

Evening ◯
Daytime ◯

Face
Moisturizer

_____

Concealer

_____

Foundation

_____

Highlight/Blush

_____

Eyes

Brows

_____

Eyelid

_____

Liner

_____

Crease

_____

Mascara

_____

Lips

Liner

_____

Lip Color

_____

Gloss

_____

Notes

Name of Look _____

Evening ○
Daytime ○

Face

Moisturizer

Concealer

Foundation

Highlight/Blush

Eyes

Brows

Eyelid

Liner

Crease

Mascara

Lips

Liner

Lip Color

Gloss

Notes

Name of Look _____

Evening ⚪
Daytime ⚪

Face

Moisturizer

_____

Concealer

_____

Foundation

_____

Highlight/Blush

_____

Eyes

Brows

_____

Eyelid

_____

Liner

_____

Crease

_____

Mascara

_____

Lips

Liner

_____

Lip Color

_____

Gloss

_____

Notes

Name of Look _____

Evening ○
Daytime ○

Face
Moisturizer

_____

Concealer

_____

Foundation

_____

Highlight/Blush

_____

Eyes   **Lips**
Brows   Liner

_____   _____

Eyelid   Lip Color

_____   _____

Liner   Gloss

_____   _____

Crease

_____

Mascara

_____

Notes

Name of Look _____

Evening ○
Daytime ○

Face

Moisturizer

_____

Concealer

_____

Foundation

_____

Highlight/Blush

_____

Eyes

Brows

_____

Eyelid

_____

Liner

_____

Crease

_____

Mascara

_____

Lips

Liner

_____

Lip Color

_____

Gloss

_____

Notes

Name of Look _____

Evening ◯
Daytime ◯

Face
Moisturizer

Concealer

Foundation

Highlight/Blush

Eyes
Brows

Eyelid

Liner

Crease

Mascara

Lips
Liner

Lip Color

Gloss

Notes

Name of Look _____

Evening ○
Daytime ○

Face

Moisturizer

_____

Concealer

_____

Foundation

_____

Highlight/Blush

_____

Eyes

Brows

_____

Eyelid

_____

Liner

_____

Crease

_____

Mascara

_____

Lips

Liner

_____

Lip Color

_____

Gloss

_____

Notes

Name of Look _____

Evening ◯
Daytime ◯

Face
Moisturizer

_____

Concealer

_____

Foundation

_____

Highlight/Blush

_____

Eyes
Brows

_____

Eyelid

_____

Liner

_____

Crease

_____

Mascara

_____

Lips
Liner

_____

Lip Color

_____

Gloss

_____

Notes

Name of Look _____

Evening ⃝
Daytime ⃝

Face

Moisturizer

_____

Concealer

_____

Foundation

_____

Highlight/Blush

_____

Eyes

Brows

_____

Eyelid

_____

Liner

_____

Crease

_____

Mascara

_____

Lips

Liner

_____

Lip Color

_____

Gloss

_____

Notes

Name of Look _____

Evening ○
Daytime ○

Face

Moisturizer

_____

Concealer

_____

Foundation

_____

Highlight/Blush

_____

Eyes

Brows

_____

Eyelid

_____

Liner

_____

Crease

_____

Mascara

_____

Lips

Liner

_____

Lip Color

_____

Gloss

_____

Notes

Name of Look _____

Evening ○
Daytime ○

Face

Moisturizer

_____

Concealer

_____

Foundation

_____

Highlight/Blush

_____

Eyes

Brows

_____

Eyelid

_____

Liner

_____

Crease

_____

Mascara

_____

Lips

Liner

_____

Lip Color

_____

Gloss

_____

Notes

Name of Look _____

Evening ○
Daytime ○

Face
Moisturizer
_____

Concealer
_____

Foundation
_____

Highlight/Blush
_____

Eyes
Brows
_____

Eyelid
_____

Liner
_____

Crease
_____

Mascara
_____

Lips
Liner
_____

Lip Color
_____

Gloss
_____

Notes

Name of Look _____

Evening ⬭
Daytime ⬭

Face
Moisturizer

_____

Concealer

_____

Foundation

_____

Highlight/Blush

_____

Eyes

Brows

_____

Eyelid

_____

Liner

_____

Crease

_____

Mascara

_____

Lips

Liner

_____

Lip Color

_____

Gloss

_____

Notes

Name of Look _____

Evening ◯
Daytime ◯

Face
Moisturizer
_____

Concealer
_____

Foundation
_____

Highlight/Blush
_____

Eyes
Brows
_____

Eyelid
_____

Liner
_____

Crease
_____

Mascara
_____

Lips
Liner
_____

Lip Color
_____

Gloss
_____

Notes

Name of Look _____

Evening ○
Daytime ○

Face

Moisturizer
_____

Concealer
_____

Foundation
_____

Highlight/Blush
_____

Eyes

Brows
_____

Eyelid
_____

Liner
_____

Crease
_____

Mascara
_____

Lips

Liner
_____

Lip Color
_____

Gloss
_____

Notes

Name of Look _____

Evening ◯
Daytime ◯

Face

Moisturizer
_____

Concealer
_____

Foundation
_____

Highlight/Blush
_____

Eyes

Brows
_____

Eyelid
_____

Liner
_____

Crease
_____

Mascara
_____

Lips

Liner
_____

Lip Color
_____

Gloss
_____

Notes

Name of Look _____

Evening ○
Daytime ○

Face
Moisturizer

Concealer

Foundation

Highlight/Blush

Eyes
Brows

Eyelid

Liner

Crease

Mascara

Lips
Liner

Lip Color

Gloss

Notes

Name of Look _____

Evening ○
Daytime ○

Face

Moisturizer

_____

Concealer

_____

Foundation

_____

Highlight/Blush

_____

Eyes

Brows

_____

Eyelid

_____

Liner

_____

Crease

_____

Mascara

_____

Lips

Liner

_____

Lip Color

_____

Gloss

_____

Notes

Name of Look _____

Evening ○
Daytime ○

Face

Moisturizer

_____

Concealer

_____

Foundation

_____

Highlight/Blush

_____

Eyes

Brows

_____

Eyelid

_____

Liner

_____

Crease

_____

Mascara

_____

Lips

Liner

_____

Lip Color

_____

Gloss

_____

Notes

Name of Look _____

Evening ◯
Daytime ◯

Face
Moisturizer
_____

Concealer
_____

Foundation
_____

Highlight/Blush
_____

Eyes
Brows
_____

Eyelid
_____

Liner
_____

Crease
_____

Mascara
_____

Lips
Liner
_____

Lip Color
_____

Gloss
_____

Notes

Name of Look _____

Evening ⚪
Daytime ⚪

Face
Moisturizer
_____

Concealer
_____

Foundation
_____

Highlight/Blush
_____

Eyes

Brows
_____

Eyelid
_____

Liner
_____

Crease
_____

Mascara
_____

Lips

Liner
_____

Lip Color
_____

Gloss
_____

Notes

Name of Look _____

Evening ○
Daytime ○

Face

Moisturizer

Concealer

Foundation

Highlight/Blush

Eyes

Brows

Eyelid

Liner

Crease

Mascara

Lips

Liner

Lip Color

Gloss

Notes

Name of Look _____

Evening ○
Daytime ○

Face
Moisturizer

_____

Concealer

_____

Foundation

_____

Highlight/Blush

_____

Eyes
Brows

_____

Eyelid

_____

Liner

_____

Crease

_____

Mascara

_____

Lips
Liner

_____

Lip Color

_____

Gloss

_____

Notes

Name of Look _____

Evening ◯
Daytime ◯

Face

Moisturizer

_____

Concealer

_____

Foundation

_____

Highlight/Blush

_____

Eyes

Brows

_____

Eyelid

_____

Liner

_____

Crease

_____

Mascara

_____

Lips

Liner

_____

Lip Color

_____

Gloss

_____

Notes

Name of Look _____

Evening ○
Daytime ○

Face
Moisturizer

_____

Concealer

_____

Foundation

_____

Highlight/Blush

_____

Eyes

Brows

_____

Eyelid

_____

Liner

_____

Crease

_____

Mascara

_____

Lips

Liner

_____

Lip Color

_____

Gloss

_____

Notes

Name of Look _____

Evening ◯
Daytime ◯

Face
Moisturizer

_____

Concealer

_____

Foundation

_____

Highlight/Blush

_____

Eyes   **Lips**
Brows   Liner   **Notes**

_____   _____

Eyelid   Lip Color

_____   _____

Liner   Gloss

_____   _____

Crease

_____

Mascara

_____

Name of Look _____

Evening ○
Daytime ○

Face
Moisturizer
_____

Concealer
_____

Foundation
_____

Highlight/Blush
_____

Eyes
Brows
_____

Eyelid
_____

Liner
_____

Crease
_____

Mascara
_____

Lips
Liner
_____

Lip Color
_____

Gloss
_____

Notes

Name of Look _____

Evening ○
Daytime ○

Face

Moisturizer

_____

Concealer

_____

Foundation

_____

Highlight/Blush

_____

Eyes

Brows

_____

Eyelid

_____

Liner

_____

Crease

_____

Mascara

_____

Lips

Liner

_____

Lip Color

_____

Gloss

_____

Notes

Name of Look _____

Evening ◯
Daytime ◯

Face
Moisturizer

_____

Concealer

_____

Foundation

_____

Highlight/Blush

_____

Eyes
Brows

_____

Eyelid

_____

Liner

_____

Crease

_____

Mascara

_____

Lips
Liner

_____

Lip Color

_____

Gloss

_____

Notes

Name of Look _____

Evening ⚪
Daytime ⚪

Face
Moisturizer

_____

Concealer

_____

Foundation

_____

Highlight/Blush

_____

Eyes   **Lips**
Brows   Liner

_____   _____

Eyelid   Lip Color

_____   _____

Liner   Gloss

_____   _____

Crease

_____

Mascara

_____

Notes

Name of Look _____

Evening ○
Daytime ○

Face
Moisturizer

_____

Concealer

_____

Foundation

_____

Highlight/Blush

_____

Eyes
Brows

_____

Eyelid

_____

Liner

_____

Crease

_____

Mascara

_____

Lips
Liner

_____

Lip Color

_____

Gloss

_____

Notes

Name of Look _____

Evening ○
Daytime ○

Face
Moisturizer

_____

Concealer

_____

Foundation

_____

Highlight/Blush

_____

Eyes
Brows

_____

Eyelid

_____

Liner

_____

Crease

_____

Mascara

_____

Lips
Liner

_____

Lip Color

_____

Gloss

_____

Notes

Name of Look _____

Evening ◯
Daytime ◯

Face

Moisturizer

Concealer

Foundation

Highlight/Blush

Eyes

Brows

Eyelid

Liner

Crease

Mascara

Lips

Liner

Lip Color

Gloss

Notes

Name of Look _____

Evening ○
Daytime ○

Face

Moisturizer

_____

Concealer

_____

Foundation

_____

Highlight/Blush

_____

Eyes

Brows

_____

Eyelid

_____

Liner

_____

Crease

_____

Mascara

_____

Lips

Liner

_____

Lip Color

_____

Gloss

_____

Notes

Name of Look _____

Evening ○
Daytime ○

Face
Moisturizer

_____

Concealer

_____

Foundation

_____

Highlight/Blush

_____

Eyes
Brows

_____

Eyelid

_____

Liner

_____

Crease

_____

Mascara

_____

Lips
Liner

_____

Lip Color

_____

Gloss

_____

Notes

Name of Look _____

Evening ○
Daytime ○

Face

Moisturizer
_____

Concealer
_____

Foundation
_____

Highlight/Blush
_____

Eyes

Brows
_____

Eyelid
_____

Liner
_____

Crease
_____

Mascara
_____

Lips

Liner
_____

Lip Color
_____

Gloss
_____

Notes

Name of Look _____

Evening ○
Daytime ○

Face

Moisturizer

_____

Concealer

_____

Foundation

_____

Highlight/Blush

_____

Eyes

Brows

_____

Eyelid

_____

Liner

_____

Crease

_____

Mascara

_____

Lips

Liner

_____

Lip Color

_____

Gloss

_____

Notes

Name of Look _____

Evening ○
Daytime ○

Face

Moisturizer

_____

Concealer

_____

Foundation

_____

Highlight/Blush

_____

Eyes

Brows

_____

Eyelid

_____

Liner

_____

Crease

_____

Mascara

_____

Lips

Liner

_____

Lip Color

_____

Gloss

_____

Notes

Name of Look _____

Evening ○
Daytime ○

Face
Moisturizer

_____

Concealer

_____

Foundation

_____

Highlight/Blush

_____

Eyes

Brows

_____

Eyelid

_____

Liner

_____

Crease

_____

Mascara

_____

Lips

Liner

_____

Lip Color

_____

Gloss

_____

Notes

Name of Look _____

Evening ○
Daytime ○

Face
Moisturizer

_____

Concealer

_____

Foundation

_____

Highlight/Blush

_____

Eyes

Brows

_____

Eyelid

_____

Liner

_____

Crease

_____

Mascara

_____

Lips

Liner

_____

Lip Color

_____

Gloss

_____

Notes

Name of Look _____

Evening ○
Daytime ○

Face
Moisturizer

_____

Concealer

_____

Foundation

_____

Highlight/Blush

_____

Eyes
Brows

_____

Eyelid

_____

Liner

_____

Crease

_____

Mascara

_____

Lips
Liner

_____

Lip Color

_____

Gloss

_____

Notes

Name of Look _____

Evening ○
Daytime ○

Face

Moisturizer

_____

Concealer

_____

Foundation

_____

Highlight/Blush

_____

Eyes

Brows

_____

Eyelid

_____

Liner

_____

Crease

_____

Mascara

_____

Lips

Liner

_____

Lip Color

_____

Gloss

_____

Notes

Name of Look _____

Evening ⃝
Daytime ⃝

Face

Moisturizer

_____

Concealer

_____

Foundation

_____

Highlight/Blush

_____

Eyes

Brows

_____

Eyelid

_____

Liner

_____

Crease

_____

Mascara

_____

Lips

Liner

_____

Lip Color

_____

Gloss

_____

Notes

Name of Look _____

Evening ◯
Daytime ◯

Face
Moisturizer

_____

Concealer

_____

Foundation

_____

Highlight/Blush

_____

Eyes
Brows

_____

Eyelid

_____

Liner

_____

Crease

_____

Mascara

_____

Lips
Liner

_____

Lip Color

_____

Gloss

_____

Notes

Name of Look _____

Evening ○
Daytime ○

Face

Moisturizer

_____

Concealer

_____

Foundation

_____

Highlight/Blush

_____

Eyes

Brows

_____

Eyelid

_____

Liner

_____

Crease

_____

Mascara

_____

Lips

Liner

_____

Lip Color

_____

Gloss

_____

Notes

Name of Look _____

Evening ○
Daytime ○

Face

Moisturizer

_____

Concealer

_____

Foundation

_____

Highlight/Blush

_____

Eyes

Brows

_____

Eyelid

_____

Liner

_____

Crease

_____

Mascara

_____

Lips

Liner

_____

Lip Color

_____

Gloss

_____

Notes

Name of Look _____

Evening ◯
Daytime ◯

Face

Moisturizer

_____

Concealer

_____

Foundation

_____

Highlight/Blush

_____

Eyes

Brows

_____

Eyelid

_____

Liner

_____

Crease

_____

Mascara

_____

Lips

Liner

_____

Lip Color

_____

Gloss

_____

Notes

Name of Look _____

Evening ○
Daytime ○

Face

Moisturizer

_____

Concealer

_____

Foundation

_____

Highlight/Blush

_____

Eyes

Brows

_____

Eyelid

_____

Liner

_____

Crease

_____

Mascara

_____

Lips

Liner

_____

Lip Color

_____

Gloss

_____

Notes

Name of Look _____

Evening ○
Daytime ○

Face
Moisturizer

_____

Concealer

_____

Foundation

_____

Highlight/Blush

_____

Eyes
Brows

_____

Eyelid

_____

Liner

_____

Crease

_____

Mascara

_____

Lips
Liner

_____

Lip Color

_____

Gloss

_____

Notes

Name of Look _____

Evening ◯
Daytime ◯

Face
Moisturizer

_____

Concealer

_____

Foundation

_____

Highlight/Blush

_____

Eyes

Brows

_____

Eyelid

_____

Liner

_____

Crease

_____

Mascara

_____

Lips

Liner

_____

Lip Color

_____

Gloss

_____

Notes

Name of Look _____

Evening ○
Daytime ○

Face

Moisturizer

_____

Concealer

_____

Foundation

_____

Highlight/Blush

_____

Eyes

Brows

_____

Eyelid

_____

Liner

_____

Crease

_____

Mascara

_____

Lips

Liner

_____

Lip Color

_____

Gloss

_____

Notes

Name of Look _____

Evening ⭕
Daytime ⭕

Face
Moisturizer

_____

Concealer

_____

Foundation

_____

Highlight/Blush

_____

Eyes
Brows

_____

Eyelid

_____

Liner

_____

Crease

_____

Mascara

_____

Lips
Liner

_____

Lip Color

_____

Gloss

_____

Notes

Name of Look _____

Evening ○
Daytime ○

Face

Moisturizer

_____

Concealer

_____

Foundation

_____

Highlight/Blush

_____

Eyes

Brows

_____

Eyelid

_____

Liner

_____

Crease

_____

Mascara

_____

Lips

Liner

_____

Lip Color

_____

Gloss

_____

Notes

Name of Look _____

Evening ◯
Daytime ◯

Face

Moisturizer

_____

Concealer

_____

Foundation

_____

Highlight/Blush

_____

Eyes

Brows

_____

Eyelid

_____

Liner

_____

Crease

_____

Mascara

_____

Lips

Liner

_____

Lip Color

_____

Gloss

_____

Notes

Name of Look _____

Evening ◯
Daytime ◯

Face

Moisturizer

_____

Concealer

_____

Foundation

_____

Highlight/Blush

_____

Eyes

Brows

_____

Eyelid

_____

Liner

_____

Crease

_____

Mascara

_____

Lips

Liner

_____

Lip Color

_____

Gloss

_____

Notes

Name of Look _____

Evening ◯
Daytime ◯

Face
Moisturizer
_____

Concealer
_____

Foundation
_____

Highlight/Blush
_____

Eyes
Brows
_____

Eyelid
_____

Liner
_____

Crease
_____

Mascara
_____

Lips
Liner
_____

Lip Color
_____

Gloss
_____

Notes

Name of Look _____

Evening ○
Daytime ○

Face
Moisturizer

_____

Concealer

_____

Foundation

_____

Highlight/Blush

_____

Eyes
Brows

_____

Eyelid

_____

Liner

_____

Crease

_____

Mascara

_____

Lips
Liner

_____

Lip Color

_____

Gloss

_____

Notes

Name of Look _____

Evening ○
Daytime ○

Face

Moisturizer

_____

Concealer

_____

Foundation

_____

Highlight/Blush

_____

Eyes

Brows

_____

Eyelid

_____

Liner

_____

Crease

_____

Mascara

_____

Lips

Liner

_____

Lip Color

_____

Gloss

_____

Notes

Name of Look _____

Evening ○
Daytime ○

Face

Moisturizer

_____

Concealer

_____

Foundation

_____

Highlight/Blush

_____

Eyes

Brows

_____

Eyelid

_____

Liner

_____

Crease

_____

Mascara

_____

Lips

Liner

_____

Lip Color

_____

Gloss

_____

Notes

Name of Look _____

Evening ○
Daytime ○

Face

Moisturizer

_____

Concealer

_____

Foundation

_____

Highlight/Blush

_____

Eyes   **Lips**

Brows   Liner

_____   _____

Eyelid   Lip Color

_____   _____

Liner   Gloss

_____   _____

Crease

_____

Mascara

_____

Notes

[ ]

Name of Look _____

Evening ○
Daytime ○

Face

Moisturizer

_____

Concealer

_____

Foundation

_____

Highlight/Blush

_____

Eyes

Brows

_____

Eyelid

_____

Liner

_____

Crease

_____

Mascara

_____

Lips

Liner

_____

Lip Color

_____

Gloss

_____

Notes

Name of Look _____

Evening ○
Daytime ○

Face
Moisturizer

_____

Concealer

_____

Foundation

_____

Highlight/Blush

_____

Eyes
Brows

_____

Eyelid

_____

Liner

_____

Crease

_____

Mascara

_____

Lips
Liner

_____

Lip Color

_____

Gloss

_____

Notes

Name of Look _____

Evening ○
Daytime ○

Face

Moisturizer

_____

Concealer

_____

Foundation

_____

Highlight/Blush

_____

Eyes

Brows

_____

Eyelid

_____

Liner

_____

Crease

_____

Mascara

_____

Lips

Liner

_____

Lip Color

_____

Gloss

_____

Notes

Name of Look _____

Evening ○
Daytime ○

Face
Moisturizer

Concealer

Foundation

Highlight/Blush

Eyes
Brows

Eyelid

Liner

Crease

Mascara

Lips
Liner

Lip Color

Gloss

Notes

Name of Look _____

Evening ○
Daytime ○

Face
Moisturizer

_____

Concealer

_____

Foundation

_____

Highlight/Blush

_____

Eyes   **Lips**
Brows   Liner

_____   _____

Eyelid   Lip Color

_____   _____

Liner   Gloss

_____   _____

Crease

_____

Mascara

_____

Notes

Name of Look _____

Evening ◯
Daytime ◯

Face

Moisturizer

_____

Concealer

_____

Foundation

_____

Highlight/Blush

_____

Eyes

Brows

_____

Eyelid

_____

Liner

_____

Crease

_____

Mascara

_____

Lips

Liner

_____

Lip Color

_____

Gloss

_____

Notes

Name of Look _____

Evening ◯
Daytime ◯

Face

Moisturizer

_____

Concealer

_____

Foundation

_____

Highlight/Blush

_____

Eyes

Brows

_____

Eyelid

_____

Liner

_____

Crease

_____

Mascara

_____

Lips

Liner

_____

Lip Color

_____

Gloss

_____

Notes

Name of Look _____

Evening ○
Daytime ○

Face
Moisturizer

Concealer

Foundation

Highlight/Blush

Eyes
Brows

Eyelid

Liner

Crease

Mascara

Lips
Liner

Lip Color

Gloss

Notes

Name of Look _____

Evening ○
Daytime ○

Face

Moisturizer

_____

Concealer

_____

Foundation

_____

Highlight/Blush

_____

Eyes

Brows

_____

Eyelid

_____

Liner

_____

Crease

_____

Mascara

_____

Lips

Liner

_____

Lip Color

_____

Gloss

_____

Notes

Name of Look _____

Evening ○
Daytime ○

Face

Moisturizer

_____

Concealer

_____

Foundation

_____

Highlight/Blush

_____

Eyes

Brows

_____

Eyelid

_____

Liner

_____

Crease

_____

Mascara

_____

Lips

Liner

_____

Lip Color

_____

Gloss

_____

Notes

Name of Look _____

Evening ○
Daytime ○

Face

Moisturizer

_____

Concealer

_____

Foundation

_____

Highlight/Blush

_____

Eyes

Brows

_____

Eyelid

_____

Liner

_____

Crease

_____

Mascara

_____

Lips

Liner

_____

Lip Color

_____

Gloss

_____

Notes

Name of Look _____

Evening ○
Daytime ○

Face

Moisturizer

_____

Concealer

_____

Foundation

_____

Highlight/Blush

_____

Eyes

Brows

_____

Eyelid

_____

Liner

_____

Crease

_____

Mascara

_____

Lips

Liner

_____

Lip Color

_____

Gloss

_____

Notes

Name of Look _____

Evening ○
Daytime ○

Face

Moisturizer

_____

Concealer

_____

Foundation

_____

Highlight/Blush

_____

Eyes

Brows

_____

Eyelid

_____

Liner

_____

Crease

_____

Mascara

_____

Lips

Liner

_____

Lip Color

_____

Gloss

_____

Notes

Name of Look _____

Evening ○
Daytime ○

Face
Moisturizer

_____

Concealer

_____

Foundation

_____

Highlight/Blush

_____

Eyes
Brows

_____

Eyelid

_____

Liner

_____

Crease

_____

Mascara

_____

Lips
Liner

_____

Lip Color

_____

Gloss

_____

Notes

Name of Look _____

Evening ○
Daytime ○

Face

Moisturizer

_____

Concealer

_____

Foundation

_____

Highlight/Blush

_____

Eyes

Brows

_____

Eyelid

_____

Liner

_____

Crease

_____

Mascara

_____

Lips

Liner

_____

Lip Color

_____

Gloss

_____

Notes

Name of Look _____

Evening ○
Daytime ○

Face
Moisturizer

_____

Concealer

_____

Foundation

_____

Highlight/Blush

_____

Eyes
Brows

_____

Eyelid

_____

Liner

_____

Crease

_____

Mascara

_____

Lips
Liner

_____

Lip Color

_____

Gloss

_____

Notes

Name of Look _____

Evening ○
Daytime ○

Face
Moisturizer
_____

Concealer
_____

Foundation
_____

Highlight/Blush
_____

Eyes
Brows
_____

Eyelid
_____

Liner
_____

Crease
_____

Mascara
_____

Lips
Liner
_____

Lip Color
_____

Gloss
_____

Notes